WATER

A TRUE BOOK

by

Christin Ditchfield

Children's Press®
A Division of Scholastic Inc.

New York Toronto London Auckland Sydney
Mexico City New Delhi Hong Kong
Danbury, Connecticut

A family uses water
to wash their car.

Content Consultant
Jan Jenner, Ph.D.

Reading Consultant
Nanci R. Vargus, Ed.D.
Primary Multiage Teacher
Decatur Township Schools,
Indianapolis, IN

Library of Congress Cataloging-in-Publication Data

Ditchfield, Christin.
    Water / by Christin Ditchfield.
       p. cm — (A true book)
    Includes bibliographical references and index.
    Summary: Describes the properties and uses of water, its importance
to life on earth, and the water cycle.
    ISBN 0-516-22345-3 (lib. bdg.)   0-516-29369-9 (pbk.)
    Water—Juvenile literature. [1. Water. 2. Hydrologic cycle.] I. Title.
II. Series.
GB662.3 .D58 2002
553.7—dc21
                                                        2001007855

1 2 3 4 5 6 7 8 9 10 R 11 10 09 08 07 06 05 04 03 02

Contents

People, animals, and plants need water to live.

We Cannot Live Without It

Water is everywhere all around us. We use it every day. We may not often think about it, but water is one of our most valuable natural resources. A natural resource is a substance found in nature that has many important uses. Without water, our world would not exist. All living things need water to survive. Plants, animals, and people are mostly made of water.

Thousands of creatures make their home in the water. The ocean is full of different kinds of fish, otters, sea turtles, dolphins, and sharks. Ducks, beavers, and frogs live in ponds. Land animals drink water from nearby rivers and creeks.

Animals are not the only ones who are thirsty. With their roots, trees and plants soak up water

A sea turtle
swims under
water (above)
and a mallard
duck floats on
water in pond.

from the ground. Water makes our fruits and vegetables grow. Human beings need fresh, clean water to drink.

Water has many other uses. People also use water for washing and cooking. In factories called power plants, water creates **electricity** for our homes. For thousands of years, people have traveled in boats on the water. Sometimes it is the only way to get from one place to another!

Without water, it would be difficult to wash clothes or cook food.

Some people play in the water while others work in it.

For fishers, sailors, and scientists, the water is a place to work. For others, water is a place to play. People splash and swim and float in the cool, refreshing water. Athletes compete in water sports such as swim-ming, diving, canoeing, and water-skiing. Water is an important part of our everyday life!

What Is Water?

Water is a **liquid** that is made up of two ingredients—hydrogen (a gas) and oxygen (air). This special liquid has no color and no taste and no smell. Water takes the shape of whatever container it is placed in. There are three different forms of water—liquid, solid, and gas.

Water has no shape of its own. It changes shape depending on what kind of container it is placed in.

Liquid water fills our rivers and oceans. It comes out of a water fountain or a faucet. It can be splashed or sprayed.

When liquid water gets very cold, it freezes. Frozen water becomes hard and **solid**. We call it ice. Ice is not as heavy as liquid water, but it has a shape and takes up more space.

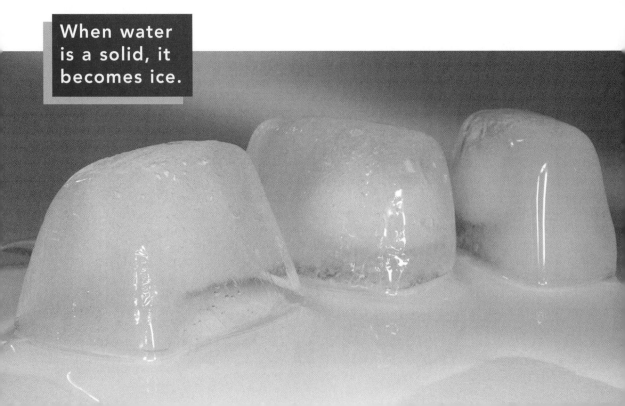

When water is a solid, it becomes ice.

Water can become a gas called water vapor. This vapor is the steam that can be seen rising from a pot of boiling water.

Sometimes water **evaporates**. It dries up and turns to gas. This gas—called **water vapor**—rises into the air. Most of the time, water vapor is invisible. It can only be seen when the temperature is very hot or very cold. Hot water vapor forms in little clouds of **steam**. You can see steam rising from water that is boiled on the stove. Cold water vapor appears like mist or fog. The clouds in the sky are made of cold water

Your breath that can be seen on a cold day is also a form of water vapor.

vapor. When you breathe outside on a cold day, the water vapor in your breath may look like a little cloud.

Water is the only substance on Earth that can be found naturally in the three different forms. It can be a liquid, a solid, or a gas.

Fun Facts About Water

All living creatures must have water to survive. Some desert animals have found special ways to get the water they need. Camels and tortoises store water inside their bodies. They can go for several days without having to drink.

Gerbils and kangaroo rats get their water from the plants they eat. Animals like snakes and lizards collect moisture from the morning dew. They lick the tiny droplets that form on their own bodies!

Water Everywhere!

Water is everywhere! Water spills down from rain clouds in the sky and splashes into the sea. It bubbles up in springs and flows in rivers. Water is in everything we eat or drink. Although we cannot see it, water is even in the air we breathe. Scientists tell us that our bodies are mostly made of water.

The human body loses water in many ways, including by sweating.

In fact, water makes up about two-thirds of a person's body weight. We lose water from our bodies whenever we breathe or sweat or go to the bathroom. It is very important for us to replace that liquid by drinking plenty of water each day. A person might be able to live for a month without food, but no one can live for a week without water!

Fortunately, there is plenty of water to go around. Water covers three-fourths of the Earth's surface. Rivers, lakes, and oceans surround us. Most of this water is salty. The salt comes from rocks and minerals

Water covers most of
the Earth's surface.

Salt water is found in many oceans and seas.

in the water. Some kinds of plants and animals can only live in the salt water of the ocean. This water is much too salty for people to drink.

The water that fills lakes and ponds is called fresh water. It does not have the salt and minerals that are found in ocean water. Different types of plants and animals live in fresh water. Fresh water is the water we drink.

A moose stands in a fresh water pond.

The Water Cycle

Although there is very little fresh water in the world, our supply has never run out yet. That's because water constantly **recycles** itself! Scientists call nature's recycling process the **water cycle**. In the water cycle, water moves from the Earth up to the sky and from the sky

Fog can be a type of water vapor that rises from the surface of the Earth.

back down to the Earth. It is a never-ending circle.

The sun heats up the water in the ocean. Some of the water evaporates and turns into gas, or water vapor. The water vapor begins to rise from the surface of the Earth. The wind blows it high into the sky.

As the water vapor rises higher, it starts to cool off. Cold water vapor turns back into tiny drops of water. These little droplets stick together to form clouds. As more droplets join the clouds, the clouds get heavier and heavier. Soon, the water begins to fall from the clouds as raindrops. In very cold places, the rain freezes and turns to snow, sleet, or hail.

Rain clouds are drops of water made from cold water vapor.

Some rivers take rain
water to the ocean.

Some of the rain sinks deep into the ground. Some falls into lakes and ponds. The rain also falls into rivers. Some rivers will carry the rain water slowly back to the ocean. There, the sun heats it up—and the whole cycle starts all over again. Water is always on the move.

What Is Next?

Water is one of our most important natural resources. Nothing on Earth can live without it. It is true that there is water everywhere, but most of the world's water is too salty for people to use. We need fresh water for drinking and bathing and cooking. Fresh water is not

Throwing garbage and pumping waste into oceans, lakes, and rivers pollutes the water.

nearly as plentiful as salt water. Some of our fresh water has been polluted. Garbage and dangerous chemicals have been dumped into the water, making it unsafe for people and animals. That is why we need to use water wisely. We need to keep it clean, and we must be careful not to waste it.

An average person uses about 50 to 80 gallons of water each day. A family goes through as much as 107,000 gallons in a year. Most people use 2 gallons of water just to brush their teeth.

Shut off the water while brushing your teeth. You can save almost 2 gallons of water!

It takes 2 to 7 gallons to flush a toilet, 9 to 12 gallons to run a dishwasher, and 20 gallons if you wash the dishes in the sink. A shower alone can take up to 50 gallons of water.

Scientists are always looking for better ways to clean and re-use our fresh water. Chemical companies and factories are trying to dispose of their garbage in a way that will not hurt the environment.

A scientist tests water for pollution.

We can all help preserve our water supply. We can turn off faucets and garden hoses when we are not using them. We can use less water in the bathtub or take quick showers instead. Remember to turn off the water while brushing your teeth. Fixing leaky pipes saves water, too. If we each do our part, there will be plenty of water for everyone!

Fixing leaky pipes is one of the many ways you can save water.

On the Job

An oceanographer is a scientist who studies the ocean. Some oceanographers measure the waves and the tides. They chart the depths of the water. Some study how the ocean affects our weather. Others look for ways to protect the ocean from pollution.

Marine biologists are oceanographers who study all the plants and animals that live in the ocean. An oceanographer's work is never boring. There's always something new to learn!

To Find Out More

Here are some additional resources to help you learn more about water:

 **Books**

Berger, Melvin and Gilda Berger. **Water, Water Everywhere.** Chelsea House Publishers, 1995.

Macquitty, Miranda. **Ocean.** Dorling Kindersley Limited, 1995.

McKinney, Barbara Shaw. **A Drop Around the World.** DAWN Publications, 1998.

Rauzon, Mark J. and Cynthia Overbeck Bix. **Water, Water Everywhere.** Sierra Club Books for Children, 1994.

Smith, David. **The Water Cycle.** Thomson Learning, 1993.

Williams, Brenda. **Water.** Raintree Steck-Vaughn Publishers, 1999.

💡 Organizations and Online Sites

American Water Works Association
6666 West Quincy Avenue
Denver, CO 80235
http://www.awwa.org

This organization is an international non-profit scientific and educational society dedicated to safe drinking water.

Planetpals Earthzone
http://www.planetpals.com

This online site provides facts and fun activities about Earth.

United States Environmental Protection Agency—Office of Water
http://www.epa.gov/ safewater/kids

The "Kids' Stuff" page features water-related games, trivia, experiments, and activities to help kids learn about drinking water.

Water Education Foundation
717 K Street, Suite 317
Sacramento, CA 95814
http://www.water-ed.org

This non-profit organization exists to create a better understanding of water issues and to help resolve resource problems through educational programs.

The World's Water
http://www.worldwater.org

A site dedicated to providing up-to-date water information and connections to many other water-related organizations and institutions.

Important Words

electricity a form of energy that can be used to create light, heat, and power

evaporation the process in which a liquid changes into a gas or vapor

gas an air-like substance that will spread to fill any space around it

liquid a wet substance that flows and can be poured

recycle to save and use over again—sometimes in a new way

solid any substance that is hard and firm and has its own shape

steam the vapor or gas that is formed when water boils

water cycle the natural process by which water constantly recycles itself

water vapor the gas that water changes into when it is heated

Index

Meet the Author

Christin Ditchfield is the author of a number of books for Children's Press, including five True Books on Natural Resources. A former elementary school teacher, she is now a freelance writer and conference speaker, and host of the nationally syndicated radio program, *Take It To Heart!* Ms. Ditchfield makes her home in Sarasota, Florida.

Photographs © 2002: Corbis-Bettmann: 23 (George Lepp), 27 (Charles Mauzy), 35 bottom (Sally A. Morgan), 25 (NASA), 13 left (Michael Neveux), 10 bottom (Joel W. Rogers); Photo Researchers, NY/Jan Robert Factor: 42; PhotoEdit: 32 (Billy E. Barnes), 10 top (Kathy Ferguson), 37 (Spencer Grant), 20 (Jeff Greenberg), 1 (Dennis MacDonald), 4 top, 4 bottom, 41 (Michael Newman), 21 bottom (Frank Siteman), cover (Susan Van Etten), 9 top, 13 right, 18 (David Young-Wolff); Visuals Unlimited: 7 bottom (Rick & Nora Bowers), 7 top (Dave B. Fleetham), 2 (Mark Gibson/ImageQuest), 29 (GLE), 9 bottom, 43 (Jeff Greenberg), 16 (Arthur R. Hill), 21 top (Joe McDonald), 26 (Charles W. McRae), 14 (Gregg Ozzo), 39 (H.S. Rose), 31 (Cheyenne Rouse), 35 top (Kjell B. Sandved), 15 (Larry Stepanowicz).